TRANSPORT ARCHIVE SERIES

THE SHAP STORY

(REVISED & ENLARGED EDITION)

compiled and edited by Gordon Baron
and Ron Phillips

Proceeds from the sale of this book will be dedicated to the
SHAP MEMORIAL FUND
for the maintenance of the Memorial and Site

First published May 1994
Second Revised and Enlarged Edition October 1998

Front Cover Picture: 'Heading for Home'
Back Cover Picture: Top 'Resting at the Jungle'
Back Cover Picture: Bottom 'Winter Time'

Introduction

Look at any map of the United Kingdom and you will see that if you ignore the M6 Motorway, there were only two major direct roads linking England and Scotland. These were the A1 on the eastern seaboard, and the A6 in the west.

The road with most stories to tell, and probably the most hazardous, is the A6 over Shap Fell in Westmoreland (now part of Cumbria). If you talk to any lorry driver, coach driver or motorist of the older generations, most of them who travelled the route regularly will have some story to tell about Shap.

Shap has become a legend. The section of A6 from Kendal northwards to Shap village, a matter of some 16 miles, began as a drovers' trail, then a pack horse track and subsequently became a road of major strategic importance. Nowadays, since the M6 opened in October 1970, it has become a quiet backwater and tourist route.

The original 1994 booklet was published to coincide with the unveiling of the Memorial at Shap Summit on the A6, which pays tribute to the drivers and crews of vehicles that made possible the social and commercial links between North and South over this old and difficult route before the M6 Motorway opened.

Remembered too are those who built and maintained the road, and the generations of local people who freely gave food and shelter to stranded travellers in all the bad weather experienced over the years.

Gordon Baron   October, 1998
Trustee, Shap Memorial Trust

Photographs

The majority of photographs reproduced in this book are from the Edith Wharton Collection (EWC), the Margaret Duff Collection (MDC), the British Commercial Vehicle Museum Trust Archives (BCVMA), or the Shap Memorial Trust Archives (SMTA). Photographs from other sources are duly acknowledged.

Photographic reproduction and restoration by Dave Lewis, A.R.P.S., of Leyland.

Copyright

Gingerfold Publications
8, Tothill Road
Swaffam Prior
Cambridge CB5 0JX

First Published October 1998

ISBN - 1-902356-04-7

Printed by Fretwell Print & Design, Keighley.

A Brief History of Kendal

by Gordon Baron

For centuries Kendal has straddled the main route to Scotland, and could rightly call itself "The Gateway to the Lakes", but since October 1970 when the M6 Motorway was opened and the new by-pass to the west of the town was completed and opened in August 1971, all the heavy lorries, coaches and cars have left Kendal to just local and tourist traffic. However, with today's volume of traffic and poor public transport, some people might say that the situation in Kendal is just like the old days. Such is progress!

Kendal was Westmoreland's principle town before the old county became swallowed up by Cumbria, the new title for the Lakes area in general. The town is a gracious place with a mix of antiquity and industry, and sits in the dale of the river Kent, which is surrounded by one of the most unspoilt parts of the country, stretching from Morecambe Bay in the south to Shap fells in the north, and from Windermere in the west to Kirby Lonsdale and the start of the Yorkshire Dales in the east. In this area you will find some of the most beautiful but underrated parts of the Lake District, places such as the Lyth Valley, Kentmere, Long sleddale and Selside. The pace of modern life by-passes these gems, and they should be left to their beauty and peace. A term often used to describe this area is "God's Own Country," and this to me is true.

Kendal was once a border town, and saw many forays south made by the Scots. Its recorded history starts in Norman times, when William Rufus drove the Scots from the north west in 1092, and then established communities in the wild lands of the Lakes. The Scots were not "good losers", and they harried the borders for centuries: as a result the lakeland communities were militarised. In the sixteenth century, Westmoreland could muster around 4,000 armed men. Of these, some 1,400 would be longbowmen, some of whom would be men from Kendal, dressed in the heavy wool cloth known as "Kendal Green". thus they became the romantic heroes of this cruel age.

The main industry of Kendal at this time was the wool trade, which had been set up by Flemish weavers about 1331, under the protection of Edward III. This industry gave the town its motto - "Wool is my Bread". Thus Kendal green cloth became famous, and was transported far and wide, and it is recorded that there was a regular trade from Kendal to Southampton in the 1500s. This trade was probably the beginning of commercial transport in the area, which was to make Kendal and Shap famous in the middle part of the twentieth century.

In 1512, in Kendal's Norman Castle (now ruins) was born Katherine Parr, the last Queen of Henry VIII. They were married at Hampton court in 1543, the King's sixth marriage, and Katherine's third. Another famous person from Kendal is the artist George Romney, several of whose works hang in the Town Hall.

In addition to the already mentioned woollen industry, other products to make their mark on Kendal were snuff, manufactured here from the seventeenth century, Kendal Mint Cake, and shoes (made by the well known manufacturer K Shoes).

The weather has played its small part in the history of the town. In 1739-40 the records state there were thirteen weeks of frost and snow, which prevented any carriers from entering or leaving the town. During the winters of 1940 and 1947 every street was blocked with lorries, unable to make the journey along the A6 over Shap Fell for long periods. In the severe winter of 1962-3, troops were brought in to help clear the roads of snow and ice. This spell of bad weather lasted for 74 days.

Today, Kendal is worth more than a brief passing visit. Linger awhile and enjoy the atmosphere of this old and historic town, for most of the buildings, courtyards and alleyways are signposted by the Kendal Civic Trust's plaques.

ORIGINS

Above: The journey starts here. The A6 looking north, in Kendal Town Centre.   SMTA
Below: Edith Wharton, who lived close to the A6, took many of the photographs used to illustrate this book. Edith and her father, who was then aged 90 years, are seen below at Hucks Bridge. The family home is seen in the background adjacent to the bridge.   EW

A brief history of Shap

by Jean Scott-Smith

Shap has been a settlement since time immemorial: this is evidenced by the once stupendous monument to the south of the village, consisting of two stone circles and an avenue of stones. This must have been something on a simpler scale to Avebury. The name of the village in all ancient documents is Hep or Heppe, and the origin of this is variously explained, 1) that the name refers to 'heap' presumably of stones (the circles etc.), 2) the old English name for the common hip, or fruit of the dog-rose. In the local dialect, which derives from the Norse, this would be called *shoup* or *choup*. We will never really know, but both seem feasable since the countryside around was littered with both the stone monuments and erratic boulders from the ice age. It was also thickly forested, of which thorns would form a substantial part. Close to Keld is a small settlement which is very ancient and bears the name Thornship, which was anciently spelt Thornshappe.

There is little of the stone circles left to see. There is partially buried circle (Shapsey) to the east of the A6 beside the railway embankment which is believed to cover the remainder of the circle. There is the remains of the resited Karl Lofts beside the section of the road through the village where the pavement is higher than the road. The stones were moved at the time of the construction of the railway, and had been described in 1844 as 13 stones of Shap Granite, the largest of which is 7 or 8 feet high, placed in a circle of about 40 feet diameter. There are few survivors of the stones from the avenue, which originally consisted of two parallel rows of unhewn stones, standing about 10 or 12 paces apart, and stretching in a north-westerly direction for over a mile. Two are the Druid Stone, behind the King's Arms, and the Guggleby Stone beside the footpath to Keld. A drawing of the structure in 1774 was made by Lady Lowther, and shows many of the stones in situ.

The ancient history of Shap is supported by the discovery of a dug-out canoe in what was formerly a shallow lake below the Shap Pink Quarry, in 1984, during gas pipe laying. At about the same time, an archeological dig was carried out above the Shap Blue Quarry, on the site of a prehistoric settlement.

The earliest recorded mention of Heppe is probably the grant of lands at the foundation of the abbey by Thomas, son of Gospatrick, in 1199. Although the abbey was of great importance, it must be remembered that there was a church at Shap before 750, thus pre-dating the abbey by several hundred years. The first stone church was constructed on the same site around 1120.

The village up until the last century was much smaller; Town Head was situated around the area of the present Memorial Park, and Town End being at the present north end of the village by the railway bridge. To the south of that village there were several scattered farms, and another settlement around the Greyhound Hotel, named Brackenber. Beyond the land was open common.

There was some building activity following the construction of the railway, and again after the foundation of the Shap Granite Works in 1865, when much housing was provided for the workforce. In 1877, the West Ward Poor Law charity built a mock Grecian building to the west of the main road, down a side road. This workhouse could accommodate 60 paupers: later it was used as a children's home. It was later purchased by the Granite Works for housing. The building, with its central tower, can be seen across the fields as you enter the village from the south; it is now private housing, and bears the name Brackenber Lodge, but the road leading to it is still called Home Lane.

Some council housing was built in the early 1950's, and more in the mid 1960's; thus the present-day Shap is probably four times the size of the original.

The opening of the M6 Motorway in 1970 changed the village forever, from the hectic days of the daily stagecoach, slower wagons, private post chaises, the passage of Bonnie Prince Charlie and his army, the runaway couples heading north for the border, through the days of heavy motor haulage to the lull of a quiet country road. But Shap still thrives.

SHAP VILLAGE IN BYGONE DAYS

Above: This 1920s view shows sheep on the highway, and the overhead telephone trunk lines.
MDC

Below: The Greyhound, a former coaching house, seen about 1900. The date stone over the doorway shows 1703, but the building dates from the previous century.
MDC

FAMOUS SHAP BUILDINGS

Above: A modern view of the Kings Arms Hotel, another inn dating from the times of the stage coach. SMTA

Below: The coach house standing opposite the Greyhound. The coach was kept on the ground floor, the staff slept above. Note the flight of steps to reach the roof of the coach. SMTA

UNMETALLED ROAD

Above: The Summit, looking north, on the occasion of the first motor cycle rally over Shap in 1900. Note the condition of the water-bound macadam. **MDC**

Below: At Hucks Bridge in 1900. The telegraph lines were not put underground until the late thirties. **MDC**

THE OPEN ROAD

Above: Strollers on the highway in the 1920s, looking north towards Wastdale Bridge. MDC
Below: All is quiet on this 1920s view looking south, with Shap Lodge standing just before the plantation on the eastern side, where the side road leads to Shap Wells Hotel. Currently this stretch is heavily wooded with coniferous trees. **MDC**

Snowbound traffic in Shap Village (above), and on the north approach to the Shap Summit (below).   **Source unknown, see page 46**

A Winter's Tale

by Jean Scott-Smith

For around five years I travelled regularly to Kendal to work, and seldom was prevented from getting home, due to the "night-watch", when the Council men parked up on the summit lay-by, and at the first sign of ice or snow, gritted the road, thus preventing many blockages.

One Christmas Eve, I had been charged with the job of getting the Christmas dinner (a large duck) whilst in Kendal, and had to bring it home with me. In the late afternoon, snow began to fall, and when I got onto the bus, we travelled as far as the Leyland Clock without too much trouble, and then we came to a halt. There was a great line of vehicles ahead. After some time, the Shap police sergeant got into the bus to see how we were (there were probably only half a dozen passengers) He then said that if we hadn't got moving within half an hour, he would transport the passengers down to Shap by his police Mini-van. However, he added that there would only be room for passengers, and not for baggage. My mind went into overdrive! What was I to do about the Christmas dinner? It would be too late to obtain an alternative by the time I arrived home. I resolved that if we had to get into the police van, I would secrete the duck inside my coat, never mind if I looked as if I were in an "interesting condition"! In the event, the traffic did get moving, and I got home by bus, but I often laugh at the time I almost had a false pregnancy. It would have made an even better story if I had actually carried out my plan, and given birth to a duck!

THE WINTER SCENE
A wartime tractor attempts to clear the road of snow drifts. These machines were built for clearing aircraft runways, and were overwhelmed by the task facing them at Shap.

Mrs. Fishwick, Sad Gill Farm

SHELTER FROM THE STORM

Above: Hucks Bridge in winter. The villagers were used to giving shelter to stranded drivers and their passengers when snow, ice and fog closed in. EW

Below: In earlier times, mediaeval travellers could find food and shelter with the monks at Shap Abbey, whose tower and foundations still survive. MDC

A Brief History of Shap Abbey

by Jean Scott-Smith

Shap Abbey was a foundation for the Premonstratensian Order, which was founded at Premontre in France in 1121 by the German Saint Norbert (1080-1134). The order had over six hundred monasteries in every part of Europe. the habit worn by this order was of white wool, and this gave the monks their common name of "White Canons", to distinguish them from the Black, or Augustinian Canons, who lived by a practically identical rule.

An abbey had been founded at Cockersand, on the estuary of the River Lune, on a grant of land from William of Lancaster, and one of its benefactors was Thomas, son of Gospatrick. Towards the end of his life, Thomas made arrangements for the establishment of a new abbey on his own estates at Preston in Kendale, but before his death in 1201, he changed his mind, and instead granted the canons a site twenty miles further north, on the left bank of the River Lowther. The place where the abbey was founded was then known as "Hepp", a word meaning "heap", and which evidently referred to the fallen great stones (megaliths) of the prehistoric circles. Within a century, the name was changed from "Hipp" through "Hiap" to "Shap", the form still in use today.

The accepted date of the foundation at Shap is 1199. The Abbey was dedicated to the glory of God and St. Mary Magdalen, and the site is often referred to as the Vale of Magdalen. The foundation thrived, and judging by the grants of further lands, was quite wealthy.

One canon attained eminence, not only in his own order, but in a wider sphere of the Church. This was Richard Redman. The buildings were extended and adapted over the life of the abbey, and one of the last additions, the tower, is the main feature to survive to this day. The end came on 14th January 1540, when the last Abbot, Richard Evenwode (also known as richard Bagot, another of the Levens family) surrendered the Abbey's posessions to the representatives of the Crown. The Abbot received a pension of forty pounds a year, and fourteen canons received smaller pensions ranging from six pounds to four pounds.

The lands were sold by the Tudor government to Sir Thomas Wharton, governor of Carlisle, and remained in Wharton hands until 1729 when the lands were forfeited and purchased by Richard Lowther, of Maulds Meaburn Hall. In 1948, the Lowther Estates placed the Abbey ruins in the guardianship of the Ministry of Works, later to become the Department of the Environment. It is currently in the care of English Heritage, and responsibility for regular upkeep has now been given to the National Park Authority.

Although the ruins are not of any great height, with the exception of the tower, the ground plan may easily be discerned, and the peace and beauty of the setting make it well worth a visit.

Shap Wells Hotel
by Arthur Bell

The present Shap Wells Hotel opened to the public in 1833, in replacement of an earlier establishment built to house visitors to Shap Wells, whose waters were said to have the smell of gunpowder because of the sulphur they contained. although they are similar in content to those of other spas such as Harrogate and Leamington. Near the hotel is a monument to Queen Victoria, erected in 1842 to commemorate her accession to the throne. The figure atop the column is not that of the young Queen, but Britannia.

Nowadays this monument can only be seen from the London - Scotland railway, but when built it was also visible from the old turn-pike road, which passed much nearer to the hotel than it does today. The present road is flanked by a plantation of trees which screens the view. The hotel was a popular place of rest for well to do travellers during the nineteenth century, a tradition which was to carry on after the First World War, when it changed hands and became popular with touring motorists en route for Scotland.

When it first opened, the hotel proclaimed itself to be ready to received the Nobility, the Gentry and the Public, but during the Second World War it was host to a different type of guest - prisoners of war. It was chosen because of its isolation. It was surrounded by barbed wire fences, and German naval and air force officers were housed on the upper storeys, with the guards on the lower floors.

It was the scene of an escape by two pilots from the Luftwaffe. On exercise walks they had seen training aircraft fly overhead, so they arranged an escape in laundry baskets. They jumped out of these as the lorry carrying them climbed up to the A6, they scrambled across to the railway, and jumped a goods train as it made its slow way up the Shap incline to reach Carlisle. Here they noted the presence of Dutch and Polish airmen from the Kingstown training base. They stole a plane and succeeded in passing themselves off as lost Dutch aviators when forced to land through lack of fuel. They took off a second time and once more had to land. By this time, the loss of two prisoners from Shap Wells and a training plane from Kingstown had been noticed, and they were arrested and sent back from an RAF base near Great Yarmouth. After questioning, they were returned to Shap Wells for the duration of the War.

As can be seen in the photograph opposite, the London-Scotland railway also climbed from Oxenholme, close to Kendal, to Carlisle via Shap. To meet the needs of the steam engine, the line was engineered to avoid the steep ups and downs encountered by the road, but there was still a stiff five mile climb of 1 in 75 to the summit at 916 feet above sea level. At Tebay there was an engine shed, to provide a second locomotive to assist goods trains up the incline, and to protect the rear of trains of unbraked wagons. At Scout Green, a signal box was provided to signal the safe passage of trains half way along the section from Tebay to Shap.

Large loads were unable to travel by rail, as tunnels and bridges were barriers. Hence the need to haul them over the road, in the early days with road locomotives at front and rear like the goods trains. Heavy haulage firms plying between the Midlands and Glasgow allowed four days for the journey, one for the Kendal to Shap section. It is even recorded that on occasions the leading road locomotive went ahead on the most difficult stretches, and then placed anchors in the ground and winched up the load assisted by the tractive effort of its companion engine. Such a convoy would be followed by the road gang, to make good damage to the surface.

SHAP WELLS HOTEL

Above: A view of the Hotel as it is today, now with dormer windows in the roof. **A. Bell**
**Below: An view in the early part of this century. In the background can be seen a London &
North Western Railway express train steaming towards Scotland.   It was from this hotel that
the only recorded escape of German prisoners of war took place in 1944, when two Luftwaffe
officers escaped and jumped a train for Carlisle.** **MDC**

Kendal to Shap Village

A Description of the A6 route by Gordon Baron

It is quite possible that there has been a track over Shap Fell since Neolithic times. There are traces of a settlement above the 'Blue' quarry which was excavated in the early 80's and a canoe of this period was found in the bed of a former lake below the 'Pink' quarry in 1984 during gas pipe laying. Certainly this route must have been established before 1199, since at that date the Monks of Shap Abbey removed their monastary from Preston Richard, south of Kendal, to its site west of Shap.The Monks established a large sheep farm,with wool from the Abbey being carried by pack pony over Shap to Kendal, which was a major wool town. In fact the farm on the site of the Abbey still remains the largest sheep farm in the former County of Westmorland.

The Bodleian or Gough map drawn early in the fourteenth century shows the road from Lancaster through Kendal to Shap and Penrith. The road from Kirkby Lonsdale through the Lune Gorge joins this road at Shap, whilst the road from Appleby joins at Penrith. Interestingly, these are the only routes shown on the whole of this map of Cumbria. There is no Roman road over Shap since there were two main arteries to the east (Lune Gorge) and the west (High Street).

The old route was in use during the eighteenth century, as it was the route followed by Bonnie Prince Charlie in 1745, but this was realigned when the Heron Syke Trust turnpike was built, and this increased the amount of traffic using this road.. It was upgraded and eventually became the present A6 trunk road. Of the sixteen miles from Kendal to Shap village approximately nine miles of the original route can be easily traced. Part of the road is tarmac as it was used as a service road to the Shap Aqueduct Tunnnel which was built recently to supplement the Manchester Aqueduct from Haweswater.

But let us trace the route as we can see it today, picking it up at the rear of the Plough Inn just north of Selside. It is fairly well preserved between the Plough Inn and Bannisdale High Bridge. In coaching days there was an Inn called the Bay Horse. The bridges on this route date from the l7th Century. From the bridge and after Thorn Cottage the road takes a sharp turn left, skirts the hill behind Forest Hall and comes out on the present A6 at Jungle Cafe. Just after the Cafe the road now branches to the left and climbs up the hill to pass left of Hollowgate Farm, thence over the hill and down to High Borrow Bridge. Various artifacts, such as a Highlander's purse and a cannonball, probably from the retreat of Bonnie Prince Charlie's followers on their journey North in 1745 have been found here. At Clifton, south of Penrith, they were to meet up with the Duke of Cumberland's army and there was a brief skirmish.

The road now follows Crookdale Beck, with the present road high up on our right. We now come to Crookdale Bridge at Hause Foot and the road climbs steeply from this point to the summit of the route.

The old road now crosses the A6 near the Television repeater station and heads north easterly to pass the ruins of Demming's Resthouse. This was probably a small Inn where travellers could rest after their climb from Kendal or Shap Village. The road at this point passes Pack Horse Hill and heads north to join the A6 again to the north of Old Wasdale Bridge

We leave the A6 again and cross the road to the Shap Wells Hotel continuing until we pass through what is now the yard of Shap Granite Works, after which we rejoin the A6 for the rest of the way to Shap Village. The Shap Wells Hotel was built to accommodate guests visiting the Wells for the mineral waters (see previous page).

A traveller from Carlisle in 1654 remarked that the road was *no other than climbing the stony'* (sic) but even as the road covered was arduous it must have been more direct, easier or safer to travel than the old Roman Road which went from Kendal to Penrith via Meal Bank, Patton Bridge, Whinfell, Low Borrow Bridge (where the Romans had a fort) thence through the Lune Gorge to Tebay and Crosby Ravensworth Fell to Oddendale, Newby and Penrith.

16

HUCKS BRIDGE, 1938

Above: A loaded Leyland "Lynx" lorry of Randall's Transport heads north. It is followed by a very heavily loaded Saurer.   BCVMA

Below: The same truck from a different angle. These pictures were taken to publicise the then new model, built to be able to travel at the newly introduced 30 m.p.h. maximum speed limit for lighter commercial vehicles.   BCVMA

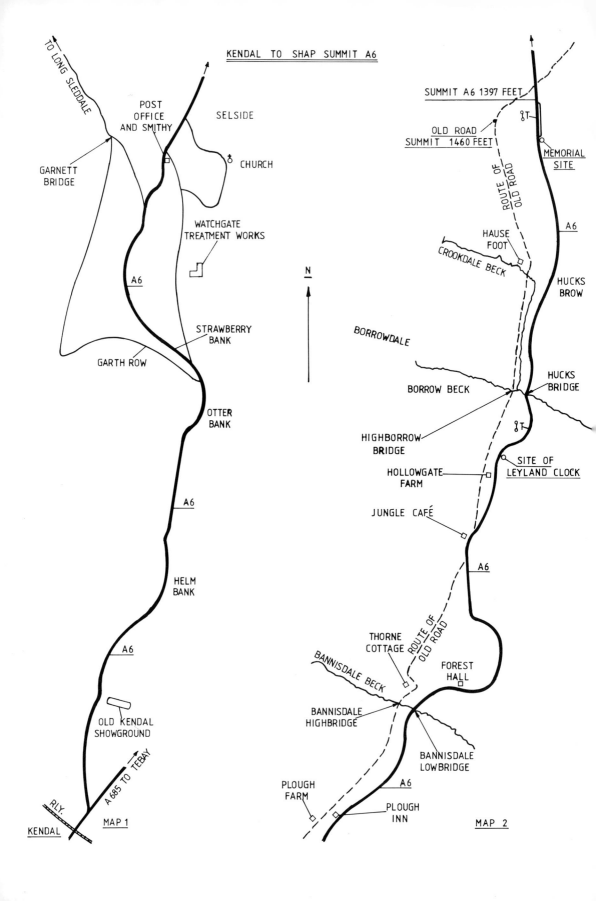

KENDAL TO SHAP SUMMIT A6

TO LONG SLEDDALE

GARNETT BRIDGE

POST OFFICE AND SMITHY

SELSIDE

CHURCH

WATCHGATE TREATMENT WORKS

A6

STRAWBERRY BANK

GARTH ROW

N

OTTER BANK

A6

HELM BANK

A6

OLD KENDAL SHOWGROUND

A 685 TO TEBAY

RLY.

KENDAL

MAP 1

SUMMIT A6 1397 FEET

OLD ROAD SUMMIT 1460 FEET

ROUTE OF OLD ROAD

MEMORIAL SITE

A6

HAUSE FOOT

CROOKDALE BECK

HUCKS BROW

BORROWDALE

BORROW BECK

HUCKS BRIDGE

HIGHBORROW BRIDGE

SITE OF LEYLAND CLOCK

HOLLOWGATE FARM

JUNGLE CAFÉ

A6

ROUTE OF OLD ROAD

THORNE COTTAGE

FOREST HALL

BANNISDALE BECK

BANNISDALE HIGHBRIDGE

BANNISDALE LOWBRIDGE

A6

PLOUGH FARM

PLOUGH INN

MAP 2

SHAP SUMMIT TO SHAP VILLAGE

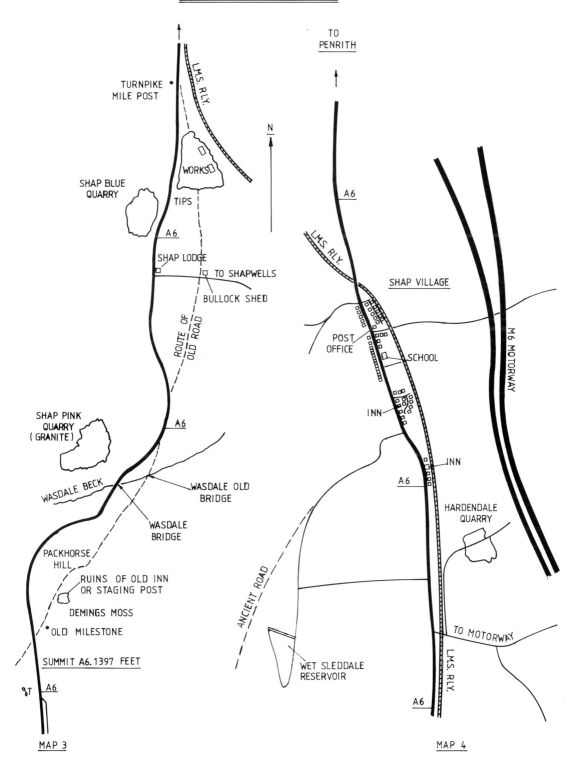

TO PENRITH

TURNPIKE MILE POST

N

LMS. RLY.

WORKS

SHAP BLUE QUARRY

TIPS

A6

A6

SHAP LODGE

TO SHAPWELLS

BULLOCK SHED

LMS. RLY.

SHAP VILLAGE

ROUTE OF OLD ROAD

POST OFFICE

SCHOOL

M6 MOTORWAY

SHAP PINK QUARRY (GRANITE)

A6

INN

WASDALE BECK

WASDALE OLD BRIDGE

INN

A6

WASDALE BRIDGE

HARDENDALE QUARRY

PACKHORSE HILL

RUINS OF OLD INN OR STAGING POST

ANCIENT ROAD

DEMINGS MOSS

OLD MILESTONE

TO MOTORWAY

SUMMIT A6. 1397 FEET

WET SLEDDALE RESERVOIR

LMS. RLY.

A6

A6

MAP 3

MAP 4

Our route was probably developed because travellers in the past always kept to the high ground as far as possible so as to see other travellers at a distance and to make sure they could keep a weather eye open for highwaymen and robbers.

The Route Today

The existing road is the old turnpike road, dating from 1764, but probably came into its own during and after the First World War. This was when goods were really starting to move by mechanical transport, which could of course carry more than the pack horses, bullock carts and fly carts of the 18th and 19th Centuries. In the 1920's the road began to develop into a major route for commercial traffic between England and Scotland. At its peak the road would be used by around 9000 vehicles a day, so we can see it was of major economic and strategic importance to the economies of the North of England and Scotland

Several ways were put forward to improve the route before the advent of the concept of Motorways. One idea was that at Borrow Beck the road could be spanned by a high girder like construction which would take vehicles directly to the top of Huck s Brow and gently to the Summit without them having to go down into the dip and then climb out again. Another proposal was for a steel and concrete structure to carry the road over the main line railway through the Lune Gorge. In 1970 nearly all the local and tourist traffic was drawn away from the A6 with the opening of the M6. However let us take a journey over the A6 from Kendal to Shap Village.

As we leave Kendal on the A6, the road is straight and flat with an industrial estate on the left and a supermarket on the right on what used to be Kendal Showground. Approximately one and three quarter miles after the showground we come to a left hand bend and immediately face the first of the climbs, up Strawberry Bank. The older drivers will tell you that if you cannot get up Strawberry Bank you will not get over Shap - so turn back!. Views to the left of us are across to Kendal and Burneside. At the top of the hill the road sweeps gently to the right, passing on the left the sign to Long Sleddale. We are now entering the district of Selside and pass the Plough Inn on the left.

After the climb past the Inn we take a gentle left turn and drop down to Bannisdale Beck. The old road used to be to the left of our route and to west of the Plough Inn, passing down Bannisdale and over Bannisdale High Bridge; the present A6 crosses Bannisdale Low Bridge.

The road ascends to the right and takes a left hand bend at Forest Hall before we descend to the Jungle Cafe, which is on the left as we swing right to climb to our next landmark, Hollow Gate Farm, on our left and recognisable by the little white windmill in the garden.As we pass Hollow Gate Farm look out for the site of the Leyland Clock, which was situated on the bank on the right hand side of the road just before we take the left hand bend.

Here again the old road passed to the west of Hollow Gate and over the hill down to High Borrow Bridge as described earlier. When we sweep down the hill, which is quite steep, passing the telephone kiosk in the layby, on the left we come to Hucks Bridge, the scene of many accidents.The bridge is often mistakenly called High Borrow Bridge which is actually situated to the west of Hucks Bridge about 500 yards away. This again is the old road which proceeds to the summit up the valley towards Hause Foot.

We now start our climb up to Shap proper. This is where the lorries used to crawl in the busy days of the 40's, 50's and 60's, and is known as Huck's Brow. It is a climb of two miles to the summit but today is a wide two lane carriageway whereas in the past it was a narrow road with a rock face on the right and a very steep drop over the boundary wall on the left. In earlier days one could see rusty old chassis, which had gone over the drop in accidents, at the bottom of the valley. The road was very narrow and sometimes lorries would have to stop to let each other pass if their loads overhung the bodywork, but it seems hard these days to visualise this state of affairs as we pass along a wide modern road.

20

"THE GOOD OLD DAYS"

Above: Selside Post Office and Smithy. Three post-men formed the establishment here at one time. The device on the left held cart wheels whilst the smith replaced an iron tyre.   MDC
Below: Coming down the hill to Hucks Bridge from the summit. A huge steam accumulator is seen en route south from Cochran's at Annan.   EW

The summit is 1397 feet above sea level. In the layby on the right there was cafe which consisted of two single deck buses back to back. As we leave the summit, the hill on our right is known as Packhorse Hill and the old road skirts this to the east and rejoins us opposite the entrance to the Pink Quarry at Wasdale Old Bridge.

We now start our long descent towards Shap Village. The road takes a long right hand bend and as we descend we can see the Pink Granite Quarry ahead of us and, after passing the entrance to the quarry we are on a more level stretch of road with coniferous woods on our left. As we travel a straight stretch we pass Shap Lodge, right, the entrance to Shap Wells Hotel. Just after this, on the left, we see the entrance to Shap Blue Quarry and to the right the yard of Shap Granite Company. After this we parallel the West Coast Main Line railway which has climbed from Oxenholme, above Kendal, via the Lune Gorge and Tebay en route to its own Shap Summit and Carlisle. The road and the railway now run side by side to Shap Village.

PEACE RESTORED
A modern day view of the A6 trunk road through Shap Village. No longer is the peace of the village broken by the roar of a constant stream of heavy goods vehicles. **SMTA**

A6 - A Shap Villager's View

by Jean Scott-Smith

The village of Shap has served the needs of transport for several centuries. The old coaching inns, the Greyhound, King's Arms and Queen's Head (no longer an inn) were built during the heyday of the coaching era. The New Ing (this is the correct spelling) which was built for this purpose with a looped drive, was never brought into use. The advent of the railway sounded the death knell of the stagecoach.

I was born in a house just a few yards from the A6 and the rumble of traffic. The flow of traffic did not decrease much at night, but became largely heavy commercial vehicles. The noise of lorries during the night did not deter sleep - unless there was a loose manhole cover in the road when every lorry wheel seemed to hit it, and the click - clack was very annoying!

Until about 1955 the A6 through Shap had a 30mph speed limit and there was a pedestrian crossing, mainly for the convenience of school children having to cross between the Boys, Girls and Infants schools. A decision was taken to raise the speed limit to 40 mph and as a result the belisha beacons and the crossing were removed. I stood in the school yard at playtimes and watched this work in progress. The area around the schools was quite hazardous, lorries used the front and side of the Boys school for parking, especially overnight. The tank trap blocks were placed around the sides of the building by way of protection. In 1956 the schools changed, the Boys school becoming a mixed primary, whilst the Girls and Infants became a secondary modern. At that time railings were put round the school front, but I believe lorries still used the north end section for parking. A transport cafe with accommodation opened opposite the school, and continued throughout the 60's until the Motorway was built..

Parking in the village could be a problem, and every level area was fair game as a parking plot. I remember in the late 40's, my home had a frontage open to the road. At times this could be full of cars to the degree that we could not step down from the front door because of cars. We later had a wall built.

In the summer months, the village became choked with traffic, especially during the Scottish holidays. The main cities Glasgow, Edinburgh, Dundee and Aberdeen had set holidays. This resulted in a mass exodus for two weeks when the holidaymakers headed for the Lancashire resorts. The traffic was virtually nose to tail, cars and coaches. Our annual Rose Fete procession always coincided with one holiday weekend and this caused serious holdups; but the collecting buckets were always full !!

As the Glasgow folk were returning home, Edinburgh was going south- and this often meant a 20 minute wait to cross the road! The Scottish holidays were not all bad - I first met my husband as a regular visitor twice a year when his family stayed at our house for bed and breakfast during their holiday. Shops and accommodation thrived during the 50's and 60's, although it was noisy and none too clean. One advantage of living on a major highway was that we had an excellent bus service, the local one being enhanced by the long distance express services.

Winters were an aspect of transport on Shap most written about, strange when you consider that this would only affect a handful of days out of the year. Southbound traffic was backed up right from the Summit through the village. The Memorial Hall would be opened to provide an emergency shelter, and the W.V.S. would provide a soup kitchen. The Police went round the village asking anyone with room to spare to provide accommodation. Any cars with female passengers were given priority of 'comfortable lodgings'.

In my secondary school days, when there was a heavy snowfall, we would be sent home - quite exciting! We would often have several days off, until the dratted bus managed to get through. Once or twice when this happened we went into school and were sent straight home again!

1962/3 was the worst Winter I remember well (although 1980/81 was severe but the M6 kept the traffic flowing). During the years 1965 - 1969, when I travelled to Kendal to work, there were only three or four occasions when I could not get home due to snow. This was largely the the result of the 'night watch' gritter which parked on the summit each night when snow or frost was forecast , and commenced gritting as soon as the temperature fell to freezing, or the snow started, thereby preventing hazardous conditions developing.

In 1970 the M6 opened and virtually overnight the A6 became a quiet village street. Obviously commerce suffered, demand for accommodation became almost non existent but the environment became cleaner and quieter. The A6 was "detrunked" in the mid 1970's when sections of the highway were narrowed by the insertion of crazy paving extensions to the pavements. The village now provides accommodation for travellers on foot - the Coast to Coast walk passes through and has caused a revival of sorts.

I end with a story of travellers for whom Shap Fell must have been an anti-climax. A couple arrived at our Guest House and, over breakfast next morning, explained that they thought it wise to stop overnight before tackling Shap Fell. My mother asked where they were heading and when they mentioned Glasgow she explained that they had in fact travelled over Shap Fell *before* stopping off!

Some Drivers' Reminiscences of Shap

1 - Kerr Ramsay - Shap 45 Years Ago

As I left the yard of Holt Lane Transport, Prescot, driving a Mark 1 Atkinson eight wheeler and trailer loaded with 20 tons of copper for Glasgow, it was 5.00 am. The Gardner engine roared into life and my young mate was looking forward to his first journey to Scotland. We passed through Ormskirk, Preston, Lancaster and Kendal. Once through Kendal the steady climb towards the summit at Shap had begun, the Gardner engine started to groan and gave an extra groan as we negotiated Strawberry Bank. Safely over that gradient I knew Shap wouldn't be a problem. We then passed a familiar landmark, The Farmers' Plough on the left; it's then that the road levels out slightly until it passes through a narrow stretch twisting and turning and just missing lorries coming in the opposite direction. We then negotiated one final bend and there was the welcome sight of the Jungle Cafe. We pulled onto the front and went inside to enjoy a most welcome breakfast.

The Jungle was more than just an eating place. It was a meeting place for all the drivers and mates to have a chat and exchange news and stories. As we left the Jungle we passed the Leyland Clock, another famous landmark in those days. My mate asked me " How far are we off Shap?". I said " Wait until we go round this next bend and your question will be answered!". And there it was, the steep dip down to Huck's Bridge and the long climb to the summit, lorries slowly coming down the hill looking the size of Dinky Toys. Going down the steep bit to Hucks Bridge I let it coast the last eighty yards or so to pick up speed. To encounter the incline you used to hit the incline doing about 40 mph, but it was only a matter of twenty yards or so before you were down to crawling speed and in low reduction gear. Once again the Gardner engine took on its groan and moan as we slowly made our way up to the summit of Shap. My mate had noticed the one or two wrecks of lorries in the valley below to our left. These had left the road a few years ago, and I told him that that was what happened when you didn't treat Shap with respect.

On reaching the summit we pulled into the lay-by to let the engine cool down a bit and check round to make sure everything was safe before we started the descent to Shap Village still keeping in low gear so as not to use the brakes too much. Air brakes were still very much in their infancy, and with the heavy load of copper we had to be very careful. We eased our way down passing the Shap Granite Works and on to Shap Village, well known for its hospitality for stranded crews when the road became snowbound. We travelled on to Penrith, Carlisle, Lockerbie and Crawford where we would encounter another famous bit of road - Beattock , but that is another story!

THE SCAMMELL 100-ton TRACTOR

Above: Marston Road Service's heavy tractor KD 9168 is seen heading south with another massive load   EW

Below: In the summer of 1934, the same vehicle is seen going north carrying a tramcar for Edinburgh Corporation. An easy haul, weighing less than 20 tons.   EW

2 - Maurice Allen - Shap Daily

In the 1950's and 60's driving over Shap was a daily task for me (this was known locally as 'gaan ower Shap'). At that time I drove a four wheeled Foden (top speed 26 mph) for Hayhursts of Lyvennet Mill, Morland near Penrith.

My journey was mostly to Liverpool to collect cattle feed from Silcock's Mill. In Winter this was no joy ride! I used to leave Morland at 3.45 am each morning which meant I was going over Shap at about 4.30 am.. At that time of the morning more often than not the road had not been gritted (no salt then.) so it was case of self service from the heaps of grit by the roadside. Every driver carried a shovel in his cab and everybody buckled to to grit the road if someone got stuck, which was frequent.

Although over the years, I never had any serious trouble there were plenty of minor incidents. One I recall happened at 4.45 going down Hucks Brow in a blizzard. A lorry had skidded crossways blocking the road. Already three or four lorries were stopped, their drivers having gone to assist the unfortunate driver. I stopped (with difficulty) and pulled in behind; as I was unladen my lorry had not much adhesion to the road. I left the engine ticking over to prevent my radiator freezing as I did not have anti-freeze in it, and got out with my shovel to go and help. The road was a sheet of ice and I fell straight away on to my back. In due course we got the road clear and I returned to my lorry to find that the vibration of the engine had caused it to slide into the back of the lorry in front! You took a chance whether to switch off the engine and risk freezing or whether to risk sliding into the vehicle in front as I had done. Luckily, due to the sturdiness of the Foden, the hefty radiator took the bump with little or no damage, but that's how slippy the road was and we had this to contend with all Winter. There wasn't much Winter comfort in the Foden with no heater, no antifreeze, a poor braking system and a smelly engine. Not the best place to be on a bitterly cold Winter day stranded on Shap Fell ! It was a case of stopping every now and then and jumping up and down to get the circulation going. The Jungle Cafe was always a welcome sight for a cuppa and a warm up, also the mobile snack bar in the Summit lay-by known as Redwing's. 1963 was the worst Winter whilst I was driving. The Fell was constantly getting blocked, a sign used to be placed in Kendal saying SHAP BLOCKED then some of us with smaller lorries would chance it going back through Grayrigg and Tebay.

The speed and power of the lorries did not match today's luxury; for instance when loaded it used to take 25 minutes from the Leyland Clock to the the top of Hucks Brow, even going down hill had to be negotiated in low gear to act as a brake. What a pleasure it was to catch sight of the Shap Granite Works when going north ,or of Kendal when heading south. Even Summer had its setbacks as the engine would overheat more than once going over the Fells. Ah! those good old, bad old days!

2 - Meikle Tennant - Reminiscences

My driving experience was with Sam Anderson of Newhouse mainly, but I also drove for William Nicholl of Coatbridge and later on for a carpet manufacturer from Bury, but by that time we did not have the snow storms that there were earlier. Shap was different because it had steeper bits in it than any other main motoring road in Britain, and also it got its fair share of snow. It lent itself to drifting because it ran more or less north-south, and most of the storms came from the east, blowing across the road.

My worst experience was one night driving for Nicholl. We were trying to get home, and it wasn't so much snow as rain that had been falling, and it formed a pebble effect on the road, and you just couldn't get a grip. It was an absolute nightmare. We had to stay at The Jungle until things turned a bit better. It was really bad, vehicles were just sliding everywhere. The Jungle was a great haven for drivers, especially when the weather was rough. But you had to be fortunate enough to be near it. If not, there were other places, farmhouses were perfectly willing to help drivers out and give them something to eat and a roof over their head.

THE SUMMIT IN WINTER

Above: The lonely approach to the summit in deteriorating conditions. A lorry bound for Scotland presses on to its destination. G.Lumb, Golcar Museum

Below: To the left of the picture, two old buses stand back to back to form the transport cafe known variously as Red Wings or the Eagle's Nest. G.Lumb, Golcar Museum

Approaching Shap from Kendal, every driver knew that if you couldn't get over Strawberry Bank, you couldn't get over Shap. Strawberry was actually steeper than Hucks Brow. It was a very sore pull, practically from Kendal all the way until you got over the top, a very serious pull. In the days when I worked for Anderson they moved some overhead cranes from Kidderminster to the Ravenscraig Steel Works, which was just being built. Some of these cranes were 110 feet long. They used some old ERF chassis to make what we call "monkeys": they had them steering because of the length. They also brought up the cross-travelling bodies for the cranes. They weighed 36 tons, and Sam's vehicles really weren't cut out for heavy haulage. To get them over Shap, some of the night trucks were detailed to double head them. The other place they had trouble with them was Beattock.

Once you were over Shap, you always felt relaxed, you just felt as though that was another journey safely done. The nightmare in those days was that the vehicles had no secondary braking.. If you lost a vehicle, then you just lost it. Today there are deadmen and what have you, if you have a broken pipe and lose air, the brakes automatically lock on. Drivers have a feeling of safety, knowing there is something to rely on. Not like on old vehicles, where if the air dropped or you burst a vacuum pipe, you could never hold them with the handbrake. Another factor was that they were very rarely running with their legal tonnage, they were nearly always three or four tons over.

Coming down, the only way to hold your lorry back was to make sure that you were down the box. If you didn't, you were on the footbrake all the time, and then you would get brake fade. That was serious, just like losing air or vacuum. You had to be in low gear, and just use the brake now and again. You never kept your foot on the brake. I've seen some who didn't know what they were doing, and there were great plumes of smoke rising from the brake drums, and you couldn't get near them for hours after that for the smell of them.

There was another way that you could try to stop them. I never had the experience, fortunately, but I do know some that had. If you had a brake failure coming down, the high side of the road was on your left, on your nearside. You could steer into the bank, just enough to try and catch the wheels on the rough. If you steered in too far, there was the risk that the vehicle would climb and keel over. The main thing was to just try and hug it enough to try and stop it.

Compared with now, the road was narrow. The maximum width for vehicles was seven foot six, and the road was about sixteen feet wide, so that left about a foot for passing. It was probably the late fifties/early sixties beforew the road was widened. I remember the widening, they had to blast away quite a bit of rock. The main hazards were overloading, brake fade, rain falling after a long dry spell, and snow and ice, of course.There were some fatal accidents. I remember one very bad one with Fisher Renwick in the late forties, when one of the drivers was killed.

When the motorway came, I was with the carpet company then, it certainly took away all the bad points about Shap .But Shap had some good points, provided you weren't fighting the elements. It was the most beautiful scenic run. It was the main artery between England and Scotland, and I don't know how the country would have survived without it. It would be quite nice if somebody could come up with the figures and amount of goods that were taken over Shap in both directions.

Drivers in the old days had to be self reliant. You didn't phone for tyre service or anything else, you had to get buckled to. There was a great deal of comradeship, you could get half a dozen drivers stopping - even though they weren't needed, they would at least stop and say "Can I help?" Nowadays, that wouldn't even be considered, because most drivers have to keep to timetables, and don'y have the time to worry about others. I would rather be back in the old days when we had time to do the job and nobody chased you. You weren't being hounded the way they are nowadays.

(Artcle based on an interview, edited by Ron Phillips)

HEAVY LOADS

Above: This Marston Road Services lorry was probably moving quite slowly when the driver steered it into the cottages at Hucks Bridge to bring it to a safe stop in 1933.   EW

Below: Two Scammell tractors and the road locomotive "Duke of York" (KD 2826) of Edward Box (formerly M.R.S.) with a heavy haul going north from Kendal. The Scammells were new to Newcastle Electricity Company before working for Box.   EW

ACCIDENTS

Above: A familiar tail-back as a result of an accident. The Shap road in 1939.   EW

Below: On the Kendal side of Hucks Bridge in the late thirties, a Bedford WTL lorry and a saloon car have blocked the road.   On the left can be seen the motorcycle and side car of the familiar AA Patrol.   EW

ACCIDENTS

Above: An all too common sight in the days of soft road verges. This Foden DG type lorry has ditched either to avoid another vehicle or because of brake fade. EW

Below: A more serious accident. This AEC lorry has met with an accident in fog and has rolled over. The roof of the cab was probably taken off by the load surging forward. EW

The Leyland Clock

by Gordon Baron and Lenore Knowles

Anyone travelling the Shap route between the thirties and the sixties will have passed the Leyland Clock situated on the east side of the road between the Jungle Cafe and Hucks Bridge. This was one of seven clocks placed around the country on major trunk routes by Leyland Motors as a way of advertising their products.

The idea for these clocks came from the then General Manager of Leyland Motors in 1930, Mr A. Whalesby-Windsor. The clocks were very stoutly made and were placed on towers some fourteen feet high. The clock face was 28 inches in diameter and the mechanism, being clockwork, had to be wound up weekly. Maintenance of the clock was undertaken by William Potts Ltd of Leeds. The clock was removed when the M6 Motorway was opened, and some time later was re-erected at the Brewery Arts Centre near the centre of Kendal.

Many people remember these clocks with affection, especially the long distance lorry drivers who used them as a reference point on their journeys. One heard stories of bosses asking"Well what time was it when you passed the Leyland clock then!?" The clocks proved to be very reliable timekeepers when, in those days, many drivers could not afford to have a time-piece of their own.

Reminiscences of a Clock Winder By Lenore Knowles

I was born in the 1930's at Hollowgate, my maiden name being Huck, one of the descendants of the Huck family who originally settled at Hucks Bridge which is also called High Borrow Bridge, and the road leading up Shap Fell is often referred to as Huck's Brow. Two famous landmarks, known from Lands End to John o' Groats, were the Jungle Cafe which opened 24 hours a day and the Leyland Clock on the right hand side of the road before dropping down to Hucks Bridge.

During my childhood my father, Thomas Huck, used to wind up the clock once a week and he received a fee of two pounds a year. After my father, I took over the clock winding for the same fee, until the clock was removed to the Brewery Arts Centre in Kendal. The man who came to service the clock was a Mr Ivor Jones, who used to stay the night with us.

The clock was a wonderful time keeper and the only thing which troubled it was blizzards which sifted fine snow into the works. I used to wind the clock in all weathers and when it was very windy I used to get wolf whistles from passing drivers as my dress blew up, often nearly over my head. There used to be a lay-by opposite the clock which was a resting place for lorries to cool off before climbing Shap. Once the mechanical parts of the clock were stolen. At my father's suggestion a notice was placed on the clock DANGER - HIGH VOLTAGE to keep people off, as the National Grid electricity pylon wires used to pass overhead. Funnily enough it seemed to work!

When I left school I stayed at home to work on the farm helping my Dad and Mam. I married Thomas Knowles, a farmer's son, from New Hutton, who came to take over the farm, also the farm at High Borrow Bridge. We have two children, Brian who lives with his wife and their two children at High Borrow Bridge and is carrying on the family tradition and Linda our daughter who married David Pigney of Appleby.

We have seen a !ot of changes on the A6, the biggest one being the opening of the M6 Motorway when all the heavy traffic disappeared, which has made the A6 a beautiful scenic route to travel. We remember many of the horrific accidents which used to happen. Ones which stand out are the whisky lorry which went over Hucks Bridge, the lorry which went over the reinforcing irons when the bridge was being widened, the runaway lorry which was carrying a tank, and the awful crash of the Harkness Coach from Penrith.

THE LEYLAND CLOCK

Above: Ribble Duple bodied Leyland Tiger coach RN 7754 on a day excursion in 1947 passes the famous Leyland Motors' clock. BCVMA

Below: Mrs. Leonore Knowles (nee Huck) of Hollowgate Farm is seen winding the timepiece, a job she inherited from her father. The date is the early fifties. L.Knowles

The Jungle Cafe

by Gordon Baron and Mrs.Flo Goodall

Drivers called this part of the district the jungle, so when a Mrs Ball opened her small cafe she called it the Jungle Cafe. Although there have been many attempts to change its name it remained the Jungle Cafe until its closure. It became an important stopping place on the journey north and in Winter it was often the furthest point north drivers could reach as the road over Shap Fell was blocked by snow. On one occasion in the 1930's drivers were marooned at the cafe for eleven days. In those times there were overhead telegraph wires and sometimes the snow was so deep that drivers could hang their coats on the wires as they set about digging their way out. However the wind would often blow the snow back again so they would have to give up and stay at the Jungle.

We come across places now and then that are famous and some that are notable, but the Jungle Cafe at one time had a notorious reputation. The influx of lorry drivers attracted prostitutes mainly from the big cities. They set up business in a collection of wooden huts behind the cafe where they lived and entertained their clients. Also the drivers would sometimes find all or part of their load would go missing. On one occasion two phospher bronze ships' propellers went missing! The day the M6 opened started as normal, but by four o'clock everything had gone dead. The cafe struggled on for a while but it had soon fried its last bacon butty and closed its doors. Today the site belongs to a firm that sells caravans and the cafe building has become offices and a comfortable room for receiving and talking to potential customers.

Working at the Jungle, by Mrs.Flo Goodall

I worked in the Jungle Cafe in the early 1940's. In about 1944 I was living at Eamont Bridge and I used to get a lift to and from work so I knew the road over Shap pretty well. Olive, who worked with me lived in a farmhouse by the Granite Quarry and used to get a lift too. A Mr and Mrs Silke ran the cafe at this time but it was owned by a Mr Geldart who had a shop in Kendal. I later moved to a house at Hause Foot next to Crookdale Bridge along the valley from Huck's Brow. I understood it was an old Roman Road. There was a track from the house which went alongside a wall to the top of the Fell to come out at the bridge on the beck opposite the Granite Quarry entrance. I then had another move to the Shooting Lodge at Shap Wells Road entrance. This has long since gone.

The cafe was always busy with lorry drivers. They used to stop to let their engines cool before and after the hill and we got to know a lot of them well as they came in regularly. Sometimes Yanky convoys called in; then the AA man used to give us a hand! They were a scruffy lot. The cafe was a mess.When they went I have seen cleaner pig sties.

The lorry drivers had the main meals, and only tea and cakes for anyone else. Eventually I got the sack because I would not work with a floozy Mr. Silke brought in off the road. But he came for me by the end of the week and asked me to work nights, which I did. It was then I really got to know the drivers well. The same chaps came in every night, up one night down the next.They always had the same lorry and they were mostly six and eight wheelers. It was not very often I did not know what they had for a load and where it was for. Youngs Express(Glasgow), Fisher Renwick ,and Holdsworth and Hanson were some of the main firms.

I never had a job to get a lift if the roads were bad .One night I waited for a lift and it was an awful night. Nothing came along so I set off and walked over. When I got to the cafe I was like a snowman! The car park was full of lorries and they all blew their horns! They had a collection for me that night. My footprints stayed on the road for days! Another time I had gone into Penrith and it came on foggy. I waited a long time for a lift before anything came along. When a lorry did appear I could not see who it belonged to and the driver did not say much so I kept quiet. We got to the

THE JUNGLE CAFE

Above: The Jungle Cafe in the early fifties. Another view of this may be seen in Alan Spillet's painting on the cover of this book. MDC

Below: A closer view of the Jungle in its heyday. Today the cafe has become offices for a caravan sales firm. MDC

Granite Quarry when the Police stopped us. The driver was a soldier who had stolen it in Carlisle. It was a long time before a regular driver let me forget. He told me he always locked his lorry before coming into the cafe. One load the drivers did not like was what they called the 'Pony Express'. It was taking dead horses to the meat shops in Manchester. One load used to be oranges for the Yanks. The driver found out that they used to play football with them so the next time he got a load he filled a box with oranges and used to throw them to any children he saw as he passed. Sometimes things "fell off the back of a lorry" but not often. One lorry went off the road near my place and was there for a few days. It was not until it was taken away that we found out it had chocolates and sugar on it! Happy days!

Keeping the Road Clear
by Gordon Baron

The Roadmen

Comparing the job of roadmen on Shap with other workers is hard to do. They worked in very harsh conditions in Winter, and even in Summer all was not a bed of roses! A nice sunny day could very quickly change to cold, wet driving rain, and on some days the A6 over Shap was actually in the clouds! But these men had to be a hardy breed, working long Winter nights to keep the road clear of ice and snow and to clear big drifts of snow in Arctic conditions such as those of the severe Winters of 1947 and 1963.

Before the Cumbria County Council took over the task in 1974, the former Westmorland County Council's Highways Department was responsible for the A6 from Kendal to Eamont Bridge. Their main depot was at Mintsfeet at Kendal, with a small yard at Bannisdale and a larger yard at Shap Village. The work force at Shap numbered some 48 men, but a lot of work such as gritting the roads was sometimes subcontracted to local haulage firms. This was done with small tipping lorries until the advent in the 1960's of the specialist Atkinson snow plough gritters, introduced on major trunk routes by the Ministry of Transport.

Gritting the road over Shap has always proved a problem, particularly in high winds when the grit would be blown off the road surface before it had time to do its job. We perhaps forget that before the universal application of rock salt as we now experience, gritting meant exactly that. Over Shap they used a combination of blue Shap Granite shale dust and sand, and Shap villagers tell with feeling of the pain and sore eyes caused if any of this mixture was blown into your eyes.

Snow clearance has always proved a problem and many types of snow moving equipment have been used. Amongst these were American *Cletrac* crawler tractor snowploughs bought from the Air Ministry. One of these was used by one of the roadmen, Harry King Cross, and his daughter recalls that it was kept in a shed at the side of their house at Selside to be ready at all times. Also used were *Mack* lorries with V type ploughs attached to the front, which were followed by the Horba snowblowers and ultimately the above mentioned Atkinsons.

There have been times in very severe Winters when the regular workforce could not cope and it was not unknown for prisoners of war to be used alongside the roadman to keep the road clear. The snow would be cut into blocks to be taken away on lorries.

The Police

The men who got very little credit for the job they did over the Shap route were the police traffic patrol officers and the local bobbies in the area. Cold weather and bad conditions made their job of keeping traffic moving under all conditions just as hard and hazardous as the jobs of roadmen or lorry drivers.

Instances of bad weather are always to the forefront of the many stories told by constables who worked this patch and the following is just one aspect of their job. One winter morning in 1941

36

MAINTAINING THE ROAD

Above: Lengthmen at work, from the Barrisdale or Shap yards. Here Aveling-Porter road roller JM 6198 is seen working on resurfacing.   Mrs.Fishwick, Sad Gill Farm

Below: Fordson trucks fitted with snowploughs were employed before the Second World War to keep the road clear in winter.   Ted Barnes collection

Shap village constable P.C.Routledge and a companion set out from the village after an overnight snowfall, when traffic had come to a standstill, to see how bad the traffic conditions were over the Fell. Once out of the village they were walking over snowdrifts and neither of them knew whether they were walking over the road or the fields as all the features were hidden by deep snow. Suddenly the snow gave way beneath P.C.Routledge, who,on being helped out of the hole, detected the fragrance of oranges. A few minutes digging provided the explanation - the drift was so deep that it had completely covered a fruit lorry which had been abandoned on the Fell!

Other memories were of coming off duty on the snow covered Fell, with his ears literally frozen to the collar of his overcoat. Motor cycle patrols in cold weather caused problems, as related by P.C.Jeffreys who recalled that when on patrol over the Fell road in extremely cold weather he became so chilled that he had to stop every two or three miles and, keeping the engine ticking over, put his hands onto the cylinder block to restore circulation and get some warmth back into his body. He would then be able to continue for another two or three miles before he had to repeat the performance to enable him to keep going throughout his tour of duty.

Another job for the motorcycle patrolmen was escorting abnormal loads. These were inevitably slow moving and on the narrow roads of the period would cause long tailbacks which had to be kept to a minimum to keep traffic flowing reasonably. But when climbing Hucks Brow, for instance, at less than walking pace, problems would be caused for other H.G.V's as they would be climbing the brow in crawler gear, so it was very difficult to keep the queues to reasonable proportions. In fog which was common on Shap Fell, the job would become even more hazardous as the traffic had to be kept moving to keep the road safe and avoid accidents.

At one time in the 1960's the Superintendent in the Traffic Department was very concerned about the number of accidents and breakdowns (mainly due to the failure of halfshafts).He decided to rearrange the patrol sectors and introduced a patrol covering the section of road from Hucks

SNOWPLOUGH
A Cle-track snowplough as supplied by America to the R.A.F. to clear runways. They proved too slow for work on Shap. The scene is the Jungle Cafe. Ted Barnes collection

MODERN SNOWPLOUGHS

Above: An American Mack 6x6 snowplough as used in the fifties. This Ministry of Transport owned example is seen in Scotland, but was similar to those at Shap   Western Trucks
Below: The Macks were replaced by special Atkinson 6x6 snowplough/gritters as seen here. These were specially built for the Ministry of Transport.   Atkinson Vehicles

Bridge to the summit, to be patrolled by one man throughout his eight hour shift, and woe betide him if he strayed off his patrol area! He was not allowed to leave his stretch of road under any circumstances. In due course a longwheelbase Land Rover was provided for this patrol which would,if possible, tow away any broken down vehicle. If a lorry broke down on Hucks Brow with a broken half shaft it caused a problem which could take half a day or more to repair, during which period it could not be moved. During this time traffic had to be kept on the move on the hill and this was at a time when the road was in its original narrow state and not the wide road we see today.

Patrol men would have to attend accidents and take care of all the consequences of them. On one occasion a patrol car was sent to an accident at Hucks Bridge and the two man crew parked their car with all its hazard lights flashing. As they walked away from the car to the accident an articulated lorry came down Hucks Brow and, as it braked it jackknifed, completely flattening the Police car! One can see how easily an accident can happen and how hazardous the job could be. One of the major accidents, and possibly the worst accident to happen on Shap, was in the early 1950's involving a Harkness coach on an excursion from Penrith to Blackpool. The driver unfortunately had a heart attack as he descended Hucks Brow. The coach left the road and plunged down into the ravine, with the tragic loss of seven lives.

There were days, however, when the patrolmen had an easy duty, when it would be possible for the them to take their break in the comparative luxury of the Jungle Cafe!

PATROLMEN

Above: Mr. Arthur Jones, who patrolled the Kendal - Shap section of the A6 in the thirties, is seen astride his BSA motorcycle combination. **EW**

Below: Mr. William (Billy) Buckham, an AA patrolman on the Kendal - Shap section in the late 1940s - early 1950s, seen passing the Leyland Clock. **L.Knowles**

A First Sight of Eden

by Peter Broadhurst

As sixteen year olds in 1947 and addicted to rock climbing, my friend and I arranged a lift from Manchester to Glasgow with the London - Scottish Transport Co. It would be the start of our journey to the Isle of Skye. After being introduced to our Glaswegian driver, who scanned our rucksacks and ropes with ill concealed distaste, we clambered aboard the big diesel. One of us sat on the engine, the other on the passenger seat.

Some conversation was attempted but was soon abandoned since our driver was obviously a man of few words, most of which began with "F!" He clearly resented having been directed to carry these young Sassenach oddities with their alien equipment. Heavily loaded, the slow diesel droned on through the night. Narrow trunk roads in those days insisted lorries travelled in slow convoy, and what with diesel fumes and the heat in the cab, we were soon fast asleep.

It would be about 2.30 am when we were shaken awake by our reluctant chauffeur who said "deyeezwansumintaet?" We said we did, and accompanied our driver into the Jungle Cafe, where he at once became animated, almost jaunty. Here, he was on his own territory. He knew everybody in the dimly lit, smoke filled cafe and after exchanging suitable monosyllabic expletives with his compatriots, indicated we were to sit down.

Turning away from us he then conducted a highly technical conversation concerning axle weights with a very aggressive fellow driver of his acquaintance. Things were fast approaching physical violence, or so it seemed, when we were approached by a well built young lady who enquired after our pleasure with arms akimbo and saying "YEP? in the manner of a potential G.I.bride.

"Geezthreeyerspecls!" said our driver without looking at her. The girl reappeared with pint pots of tea and wedges of bread. This was quickly followed by three plates of food the like of which we had never seen since 1939. Ham, Eggs, Black Puddings, Tomatoes, Kidneys, Sausages, Fried Bread, etc.,etc. The ham on each plate alone was more than a month's ration for two people and the total cost was unbelievably small.

After this feast and back on the road, conversation flowed. We were unable to translate most of it, but that did not seem to matter. Our driver was now in total control, having shown us what real comradeship was about. We stopped on Shap Summit watching dawn break over the Pennines and the Eden Valley. A steam hauled mail train appeared as if on cue and I decided there and then that this was surely God's own country and one day, God willing, I would live there.

The drive through the Borders was an anti-climax. Being dumped in the Gorbals by our now genial driver and directed to the Balloch tram seemed unreal. We had never seen drunks sleeping it off on the pavement or barefoot children running about in the streets.

I am content to live near Shap in retirement as most of my working life has been spent within easy reach of the Eastern Fells. I owe it all to that driver, Shap, and my first view of Eden.

The Shap Memorial Trust

The idea for a memorial was conceived from listening to visitors to the British Commercial Vehicle Museum at Leyland, mainly the older generation of drivers, who nearly always would have a story or memories about driving, or about journeys over Shap Fell between Kendal and Shap Village. So in 1991 the Friends of the Museum initiated a feasability study to see if and where a memorial could be erected.

The memorial would pay tribute to the drivers and crews of vehicles who used the A6 route over Shap, also paying respect to the local people who gave food and shelter to travellers in the severe weather experienced in the winter months over the years.

After looking at several sites, it was decided that the best possible one would be the lay-by at the summit of the A6 at Shap Fell, and so planning permission was sought from the local authority. It was at this point that it had to be decided what form the memorial would take, and by a piece of good fortune, the Trust was offered the donation of a large piece of rock (Shap pink granite) from the Shap Granite Company Ltd. (R.M.C.Roadstone). An appeal was launched for funds to help finance all the work involved in successfully completing the project.

In 1993, the Friends of the BCVM set up the Shap Memorial Trust Fund, now known as the Shap Memorial Trust. It was founded to help construct, erect, and maintain the memorial and site. A national appeal was launched, and was very successful. The memorial was unveiled on 7th May, 1994.

To help raise further funds a booklet entitled "The Shap Story" was published to coincide with the unveiling. This booklet would not have been produced without the support of the local people of Shap village and the surrounding district. After the success of the booklet, a video was produced, which has been highly acclaimed and is a best seller in its field.

This present book has been produced in replacement of the original 1994 booklet, now out of print. We hope you have enjoyed this second and much enlarged edition of "The Shap Story".

43

THE LEYLAND CLOCK TODAY

Above: Seen before renovation and rededication in October 1996 at the Brewery Arts Centre, Kendal, is the clock which formerly stood beside the A6 at Shap. **SMTA**

Below: The commemorative stone supplied by the Shap Memorial Trust. **SMTA**

6th OCTOBER 1996

Lenore Knowles ceremonially restarted the clock once sited at the side of the A6 at Selside in its new home, the Brewery Arts Centre at Kendal. At her side is Gordon Baron, a trustee of the Shap Memorial Trust.   Geoff Meek

Bibliography

Roman Roads in Britain, by Ivan D. Morgan (J.Baker, London)
A Pageant of Lakeland, by Arthur H. Griffiths (Robert Hale, London)
Inside Real Lakeland, by Arthur H. Griffiths (Guardian Press, Preston)
Shappe in Byegone Days, by Joseph Whiteside (Titus Wilson, Kendal)
Kendal, A Social History, by Roger Bingham (Cicerone Press)
The Domesday Book, edited by Thomas Hinde (Bramley Books)

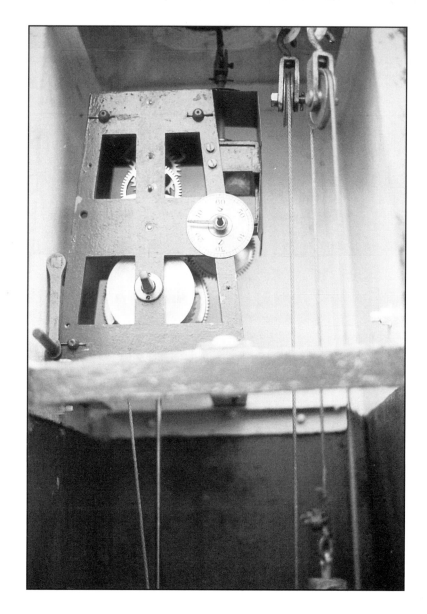

MARKING THE PASSING OF TIME
The mechanism of the clock seen here after restoration. The "Starting Handle" on the left is the crank which Lenore Knowles used weekly to wind the timepiece (see page 33)

Geoff Meek

Acknowledgements

We must tender grateful thanks to Alan Spillett for permission to use colour reproductions of three of his paintings on the cover, and to Peter J. Davies for permission to use his original drawing as a frontispiece. Our thanks also to Katy Greenwood for transcription of the interview with Meikle Tennant (pp.26-8), and to Dorothy Robinson for proof reading.

The photographs on page 10 were originally published locally by Cumbrian Newspapers, and are thought to have come from an unknown newsagency.

See this story on screen ! A highly acclaimed video is available from
British Commercial Vehicle Museum
King Street
Leyland
Preston PR5 1LE
Price £16.50 including postage & packing.